You Are Brilliant

Brilliant

7 WAYS TO SHINE

You Are Brilliant

7 WAYS TO SHINE

"Arise, shine; for thy light is come, and the glory of the Lord is risen upon thee."

Isaiah 60:1

JoLena Johnson

Be Inspired!

MISSION POSSIBLE PRESS
Creating Legacies through Absolute Good Works
Aspiration Publishing Series

The Mission is Possible.
Sharing love and wisdom for the young and
"the young at heart," expanding minds,
restoring kindness through good thoughts,
feelings, and attitudes is our intent.
May you thrive and be good in all you are
and all you do...
Be Cause U.R. Absolute Good!

Scripture quotations are from *The Holy Bible, The New Open Bible Study Edition (KJV)* © 1990 by Thomas Nelson, Inc.

Other Scriptural References are from Biblegateway.com (New International Version).

You Are Brilliant, 7 Ways to Shine
© 2015 Jo Lena Johnson
www.jolenajohnson.com
jolenajohnson@absolutegood.com

Published by
Mission Possible Press
A Division of Absolute Good
Absolute Good Training & Life Skills Management
P.O. Box 8039, St. Louis, MO 63156
www.AbsoluteGood.com

ISBN 978-0-9852760-9-6
Printed in the United States of America

Contents

———❋-❋-❋———

Thanks God!

Thank You God.

Thank You for loving us unconditionally.
Thank You for loving us for who we are
and for who we are not.

Thank You for keeping our lights burning
even when we begin to dim, and for
being the shelter, shadow, shade and
sufficiency in which we live, move and
have our being.

Thank you for allowing us to reside in You
and for being the guide, hope, springs
and source through whom we shine.

In the name and nature of Jesus Christ,
Amen

Showing Your Brilliance

We can begin to live in a manner which cultivates life as it is meant to be. It starts with a thought, a simple thought. You are brilliant. Yes, even on bad hair days, you are brilliant.

Life is not easy. Every day problems can be tough. It's easy to feel confused, lost or simply alone in today's world. You are not alone. You Are Brilliant. There are reasons for everything!

The #1 *cause* of conflict is lack of/or miscommunication. It's easy to misunderstand and to send/receive mixed messages. The *source* of most conflict is failed expectation. *Expectations happen in your head.*

At times those expectations no longer serve you. Misplaced, misguided or simply unrealistic, certain expectations get worn out and old. It's time to clear your head by checking in to see what's going on. Nobody is in your head except you; so you can probably see why others are confused since you sometimes feel confused. They didn't know and neither did you.

Confusion can give way to clarity if you are willing. You can have a do over. Just breathe.

Turn and be healed.

What does that mean? Turn your attention. Think differently, evolve. See with your eyes to perceive what's actually happening.

Hear with your ears so you may listen to what's being spoken and unspoken. Understand with your heart, allowing truth to flow like river water to the ocean. Use your bible. These are ways to radiate.

You were born to thrive. You can get past "it." In those moments when you feel discontent, allow peace and harmony to soothe, heal and calm you. Allow means "let." Let yourself "step out of the traffic." Raise your view. Rise to your own brilliance.

When we see, hear and apply goodness, we radiate and shine from within.

I've had those "late in the midnight hour" experiences like many others where I felt sad and unworthy to ask God to get me out of yet, one more situation "I created." Can you relate to what I'm saying?

At times I cried myself to sleep because I didn't know what else to do. Tempted to pick up the phone or do something I may regret, I forced myself to find ways to cope. Writing has helped me. At times I wrote and wrote and wrote letters, not to be mailed, but to express, to get it out, to help me breathe through another minute. Sometimes I started reading the bible, which made me feel better. Other times? I clutched the bible in my arms, holding it tightly to my chest, just to fall asleep, sleeping with it for the rest of the night.

Sometimes we need a bit more help – help to get us out of our little minds and into the bigness of who we are through Him.

You are brilliant. Do you know that? No matter where you are right now, what you've been through, or what you look like, you are brilliant. When having "bad hair days," we forget to see our brilliance and forget to acknowledge it too.

When we are filled with more positive thoughts about ourselves, we smile more, feel better, look better, and are more pleasant to be around. The *7 Ways to Shine* will support you in showing your brilliance!

Psalm 46:8-10 from The Message Bible reads,

"Attention, all! See the marvels of God! He plants flowers and trees all over the earth, Bans war from pole to pole, breaks all the weapons across his knee. "Step out of the traffic! Take a long, loving look at me, your High God, above politics, above everything."

If as adults, we are willing to look at the basics and review what we are doing well, not doing at all, and what we must remember to do. We can begin to live in a manner which cultivates life as it is meant to be.

Read this book, listen to the accompanying CD, surf the internet for the referenced songs, add them to your collection, and receive!

Thank you for sharing your brilliance!

"I Love The Lord"
Whitney Houston & the Georgia Mass Choir

1. Love

Start now by saying,
"I love me"
because when you love yourself, you
believe in yourself, and you know you
are lovable no matter what. Also,
loving yourself teaches you how to
love others as well.

In Isaiah 6:8 we read, *"Also I heard the voice of the Lord, saying, Whom shall I send, and who will go for us? Then said I, Here am I; send me."*

Imagine feeling lovable enough to "be sent by God" to demonstrate His mighty works!

When most of us grew up, we were taught to say "I love you" and to respond to "I love you." If you understand how much "you" matter, you will have the experience and wisdom to live extraordinarily in the face of life's challenges. Start now by saying "I love me." When you do that daily, repeatedly, you will feel loved, lovable and loving.

Forgiveness is key – letting go is a process.

Affirmation:

"My Dear Father! When I miss Your mark, please cleanse my heart, mind, and soul, as You guide me to love. Fill me and make me available to Your Holy Spirit. In Jesus' name, thank You God!"

"You Are God Alone"
- Marvin Sapp, WOW Gospel 2004 Album

2. Be Patient and Kind

When there are misunderstandings, don't give up. Learn to listen. Share your thoughts and feelings in ways which allow others to share with you. This will help you learn, grow, and you will become thoughtful and generous.

Proverbs 22:4 reads, *"By humility and the fear of the Lord are riches, and honour, and life."*

Fear can also mean "obedience, guidance, reverence, and listening." When we allow the Spirit of God to flow through our thoughts and feelings regularly, daily, and in times of stress, we are able to "show" patience and kindness because those are characteristics of Him.

"And Joshua said unto the people, sanctify yourselves: for tomorrow the LORD will do wonders among you." Joshua 3:5

Affirmation:

"I am a gentle servant in progress."

Do you want to be perfect? Most people do – and it's not possible. However, striving to live up to an affirmation in attitude and behavior can create desired results.

In service, we must be gentle, loving and kind. Although each of us has a great capacity to love, we don't always show it. Sometimes we may get impatient when things take a long time or when someone else is not "living up to our expectations." Sometimes we or the other person simply misunderstands. Just know that expectations ("perfect" in our eyes) can get us into trouble!

Learning "How to love others," can be challenging, if we are relying on our "little" selves. We need help!

Sincerely claiming an experience will assist you in getting what you really want. In this case, it's to show patience and kindness. When you say "I am" before any statement, you are attaching your identity to it, you create it, and you live it. In this light, the thing, the principle, the affirmation becomes "true" for you.

"I am" is the true name of God.

"I am" is what I mean by "attaching your identity." "I am" with a negative brings that thought to you as an experience. "I am" with a positive brings that thought to light for you. "I am a gentle servant in progress" makes it true for you, if you are willing to claim it in attitude and ultimately, with practice, in behavior.

"I am a gentle servant in progress."

Who do you say you are? *I am...*

"God Favored Me, Part 1"
- Hezekiah Walker & LFC,
God Favored Me, Part 1 (Radio Single)

3. Respect Yourself and Others

Be considerate in your deeds and actions in ways that would meet the approval of your Father and family at all times.

I Kings 3:5 says, *"In Gibeon the Lord appeared to Solomon in a dream by night: and God said, Ask what I shall give thee."*

King Solomon spoke to God, and he asked for something which pleased the Lord... Wisdom!

"Give therefore thy servant an understanding (hearing) heart to judge thy people that I may discern between good and bad..." I Kings 3:9

Especially in tough times, it becomes difficult to "hold your gracefulness." Being grounded in your Spiritual self can make it easier to be mindful of your best thoughts, feelings, actions, attitudes, and what you show to others!

In tough times, affirming this slightly modified version of Psalm 25:20-22 may be of help:

Affirmation:

"O keep my soul, and deliver me: let me not be ashamed; for I put my trust in You. Let integrity and uprightness preserve me; for I trust in you. Deliver me O God, out of all my troubles."

"God Blocked It" (Live)
– Kurt Carr, One Church (Live) Album

4. Show Good Character

Your Spirit is good and so is your nature. You get to make good choices so as you grow you will be enthusiastic, positive, and productive.

Psalm 125:4 says, *"Do good, O Lord, unto those that be good, and to them that are upright in their hearts."*

Sometimes it's great to create an affirmation or prayer, but there are so many which exist already! Here are the words of David, from Psalm 143:10.

Affirmation/Prayer:

"Teach me to do your will, for you are my God; may your good Spirit lead me on level ground."

"I'm A Christian Man"

Dennis Ross III,

I'm A Christian Man (Single)

5. Be a Willing Student

Focus on completing formal education and life lessons. Learn to discover and explore new things by asking questions when you don't understand. When you are willing, you become informed and wise.

Proverbs 22:12 states, *"Apply thine heart unto instruction, and thine ears to the words of knowledge."*

Tuning into inspiration, revelation from God, tuning out the mind, the small thoughts which keep us stuck is important and possible. This is not only true for children; it's true for everyone. As each is willing to continue learning, no matter how great or small previous accomplishments, extraordinary living takes place.

"Think big!" As you stretch your mind with the Word of God, filled with the Spirit of God, your capacity and works will be stretched by the Presence of God.

"I delight to do thy will, O my God: yea thy law is within my heart." Psalm 40:8

My Prayer:

"I am willing. Please show me how to be big and be clear in your sight oh, Lord God. Thanks for exposing me to new - Your ideas, that I might grow and connect with the extraordinary You, in Jesus' Name, Amen."

"We'll Say Yes!"
– West Angeles Church of God Mass Choir

6. Practice Personal Care

This means wash your hands, clean your face, brush your teeth, comb your hair, and dress with care; have regular checkups with dentists and doctors; eat healthy food; and get exercise too.

1 Corinthians 6:19: *"Do you not know that your body is a temple of the Holy Spirit, who is in you, whom you have received from God? You are not your own."*

When you dress, practice hygiene, choose certain foods, fail to exercise, or fail to rest, do you consider others in your life who are affected by what you do and don't do? Epidemics and illnesses which cripple and shorten life happen many times because people don't love themselves. Learn to appreciate you.

Some things are just unacceptable!

When you see young people who may or may not be related to you, what do you think about their attire or habits? What do you think those same young people think about yours?

The mind may judge but the heart of God knows true compassion. Let God radiate and shine through you!

Part of living an extraordinary life means to value self and to take time for the "little things" which make up the big things. Too many are dying of breast cancer, prostate cancer, and complications from diabetes, and other diseases. You cannot be *the gift* if you are not here to live it! Of course, it's easier said than done, but for you there is always help!

Affirmation:

Thank You, God, for filling my spirit, mind, soul, and body with what is suitable to Your taste. Less of me, and more of Thee!

"I'm Gonna Be Ready"
– Yolanda Adams

7. Put God First

Thank God for your loved ones and for all the good things in your life. When you need something, ask Him. He will always protect, support, and love you. Remember to pray every day, and thank God everyday for YOU!

Psalm 78:35 says, *"And they remembered that God was their rock, and the high God their redeemer."*

During dark times, when conditions seem too much to bear, it may seem easier to give up. Or to think perhaps God has forgotten you. Feeling shut out, cut off or out in the cold can simply be that – a feeling. It is not the Truth. God invites us and gives us an opportunity to live under grace, mercy and in faith.

In the footnotes of *The New Open Bible, Study Edition,* it is explained:

"To be Holy means to be set apart. God is set apart from the power, practice, and presence of sin, as set apart to absolute rightness and goodness."

My Prayer:

Lord, I love You. Thank You for eternal blessings, the ability to think in my right mind, and for another day to serve You. Peace be still. Thank You! In the name of Christ Jesus, Amen.

"Dear God"
– Smokie Norful

New Thoughts...

What Do You Think?

Think, say and feel, "I love me." Be patient and kind. Respect yourself and others. Show good character. Be a willing student. Practice personal care. Put God first.

Taking action is your choice. So, consider specific ways and areas in which you are willing to take action and demonstrate your brilliance. Remember, your divine purpose is extraordinary. Daily you have an opportunity to shine. You are *really* good at something. Find it. Share it. You are needed by people and by God...for the work, for...
the mission of absolute good.

Psalm 27:1 says, *"The Lord is my light and my salvation; whom shall I fear? The Lord is the strength of my life: of whom shall I be afraid?"*

I don't know about you, but I've been "pretty chicken" in my life. Yet showing brilliance is demonstrative. Imagine if we each demonstrate "brightly" each time God calls upon us to service. The concept is extraordinary! Yet, He says it's possible. *Are you listening?*

How do you typically listen?

Do you listen with your heart? Emotions? Voices from memories of the past?...

Stop. Check in with yourself and your thoughts. If you've ever thought, "I'm not good enough," "I can't do it," or "I knew this would happen," just stop. Those are the "little thoughts" keeping you from the big ideas and actions which come from God.

"You Are Brilliant - 7 Ways to Shine"

Take a few deep breaths in this moment, breathing in through your nose and releasing gently and deeply through your mouth. Feel your mind clearing and your body releasing. Begin to find the Still, Small Voice which is in you. Find your center, listening as you become calm.

Rise above the desire to stop, and begin to practice hearing what God is waiting to share with you. Keep breathing, asking for the connection, and receive what is yours.

Are you listening?

***

...He's calling you to your Extraordinary. Remember this passage from #1 Love ...

"Also I heard the voice of the Lord, saying, Whom shall I send, and who will go for us? Then said I, Here am I; send me."

Isaiah 6:8

Are you willing to answer the call?

"Step By Step" – Whitney Houston, written by Annie Lennox, Remixed by Teddy Riley on the Preacher's Wife Album

Rise and Shine!

*These and better things
shall you do.*

\- Jesus

From My Heart

—❂—❂—❂—

Like Swiss Cheese - Holes not whole is how I've felt. Too many times I felt like "Swiss Cheese" based on occurrences in my life. Body shots, words which cut like knives or deadly stares... whatever I name them, they hurt. Working, relating and living day to day, especially as a single business woman, takes more than my independent "little self" to make it, let alone thrive.

There are wounded hearts, sad hearts, angry hearts, and judgmental hearts too. I've experienced each one. Healing takes effort. Forgiving ourselves and others is part of the work. Jesus instructs us to do this, and we must. Forgiveness and trust are not the same.

Start with forgiving and notice if those from the past deserve to be in your future. Trust must be earned. At times you'll need to give up certain associations, lightening the load. Like I have learned to do, ask yourself, "Have the behaviors and attitudes changed?" If no, they've got to go because trusting is character-based.

When you listen, hearing beyond the "little self" shifts happen. Over time, you'll know as discernment builds.

Gratefulness is the gateway to happy, joyful, compassionate hearts. With consistent effort, direction, guidance, and connection to God, from within, you shine.

Giving from the overflow is key. Filling up with prayer, willingness, obedience, affirmation, along with inviting God's guidance and power to lead my thoughts, feelings and life, heals. I go from holes to whole.

I'm an avid reader. The Holy Bible is my favorite book. I write prayers all the time. Each of the songs I've listed in this book have helped me at times when I wanted to quit. I see these songs like prayers. I relate to the singers and writers, wondering what may have inspired them to create such praise and worship for us to enjoy. I am grateful to them for sharing their brilliance. You can just tell when things come from the heart.

Use what you've got – and you've got a lot – to Shine. From the inside out, you are Brilliant. Always remember that.

You are "Blessed and Highly Favored," just

as the Clark Sisters sing. I mean it. When you feel less than your best, please remember these words...You Are Brilliant! Yes, You ARE Brilliant!

From my heart.
Jo Lena

Additional Songs

I wish I could do a compilation of my favorite songs, with the words. I just had to add these to the ones I mentioned in previous chapters. They have served as powerful tools of healing, prayer, praise and thanksgiving.

Order My Steps in Your Word
– Richard Smallwood

Stand
– Donnie McClurkin

*Celebrate &
Give Me A Clean Heart*
– Fred Hammond

Break Every Chain
– Tasha Cobbs

Take Me to The King
– Tamela Mann

The Presence of The Lord
– Byron Cage

And the ENTIRE *"The Preacher's Wife"*
Album from the angelic voice of
Whitney Houston

Demonstrating
Brilliance takes effort.

It's time to do your work.

Doing The Workbook

———◦-◦-◦———

Can you sing this song? *"My Life Is In Your Hands,"* by God's Property? If you haven't heard it, you can't say yes or no! Just like the other songs shared, there is meaning "back of the words." What songs encourage and inspire you? What words are ringing in your ears? Find your meaning – dare to share your Brilliance.

It's easy to read a few pages, feel good and go... it's harder when you are in the midst of chaos, confusion or just day to day life.

Showing your brilliance is not a once in a lifetime event. Practice makes skilled, not perfect. Right now, today, you have new choices. Are you willing to rise to them?

Experience is the best teacher. Review the 7 Ways to Shine and complete the questions to seal in your luster.

#1 Love! Start now by saying, "I love me" because when you love yourself, you believe in yourself, and you know that you are lovable no matter what. Also, loving yourself teaches you how to love others as well.

What are 3 ways you can show love in action, word, deed – and to whom?

....

....

....

....

....

....

....

....

....

....

....

#2 Be Patient and Kind! When there are misunderstandings, don't give up; learn to listen, to share your thoughts and feelings in ways that allow others to share with you. This will help you learn, grow; and you will not become selfish.

Are you patient or are you an ever-evolving work in progress? In which 3 areas can you demonstrate patience – and why?

....

....

....

....

....

....

....

....

....

....

#3 Respect Yourself and Others! Be considerate in your deeds and actions in ways that would meet the approval of your Father and family at all times.

Holding to "your gracefulness" can be especially difficult during times of conflict. With certain people or situations, perhaps you could practice becoming skilled at demonstrating respect? What are you willing to do or say differently – with whom and why?

....

....

....

....

....

....

....

....

#4 Show Good Character! Your Spirit is good and so is your nature. You get to make good choices so that as you grow you will be enthusiastic, positive, and productive.

Talking, judging and thinking are nearly automatic for us all. In which areas can you make responsible choices, answering to He who counts, even when others may or may not agree or understand?

....

....

....

....

....

....

....

....

....

....

#5 Be a Willing Student! Focus on completing formal education and life lessons. Learn to discover and explore new things by asking questions when you don't understand. Because, when you are willing, you become informed and wise.

Do you act like a know it all? In which 3 areas of your life are you willing to step out of your comfort zone and stretch – and what may happen when you do?

....

....

....

....

....

....

....

....

....

#6 Practice Personal Care! This means wash your hands, clean your face, brush your teeth, comb your hair, and dress with care; have regular checkups with dentists and doctors; eat healthy food; and get exercise too.

Often, as adults, we take short cuts – leading to poor results. What are 3 habits you are willing to give up in order to produce better results mentally, physically, emotionally and/or spiritually?

....

....

....

....

....

....

....

....

#7 Put God First! Thank God for your loved ones and for all the good things in your life. When you need something, ask Him. He will always protect, support, and love you. Remember to pray every day, and thank God everyday for YOU!

What has been distracting you? In which 3 areas are you prepared to release, get unstuck and move forward – with the knowledge, wisdom and guidance of God?

....

....

....

....

....

....

....

....

Start now by saying…

I am Brilliant!

I strive to do and be my best.
God handles the rest!

Yes, I am Brilliant!

———※·※·※———

Strive to do and be your best.
God Handles the rest.
- Jo Lena Johnson, Be Inspired

Thank You Note!

———❋-❋-❋———

The purchase of this book funds hopeful writers and turns them into published authors because you are sharing your brilliance.

I was stuck on how to publish more good books without having grants, becoming a non-profit, selling my soul, or selling something else to accomplish my God-given aspirations. I priced this book so I could publish authors who do not have access or resources to do so, on their own. What am I talking about? A new venture! Profit from this book will pay for editing, design, book elements, marketing

———

materials and more – the things necessary to successfully publish books.

Aspiration Publishing Series
STRATEGIES FOR LIFE'S PROBLEMS

For those who have a strong desire to achieve something high or great.

The Aspiration Publishing Series offers Strategies for Life's Problems because we need each other and deserve access. A "Hub for Healing," you'll find resources to help you get out, get up, move through, rise above, move forward, get unstuck and have some guidance, direction, support, answers and maybe even a plan.

Need more?

Sometimes you have to see and live through the bad and the ugly to uncover to the good. We care enough to share truth - our truth & The Truth. If you are sad, mad or

---

in pain; desire a change or need healing; or simply seeking choices or solutions, we made it through and so can you!

Why the Aspiration Publishing Series?

Life is not easy. Secrets often prevail. Truth fades to the background and families suffer. People have stories to tell which are at times raw, real, unnerving and even sad. Yet each story is inspirational. With age and life comes baggage. How a person deals with their baggage can mean death or life. These authors have shown themselves to be, if nothing else, *Aspirers*. Aspiration means a strong desire to achieve something high or great.

During the most devastating times something high or great could be as simple as not answering "that" telephone call or "walking away" to save a life. By sharing their stories and how they made it through, others can be encouraged, enlightened and perhaps even motivated to make it through their own situations.

***Stories/subjects are real. Names may be changed or altered to protect the innocent & not so innocent in certain cases.

To contribute stories, purchase more books or to simply support this endeavor, contact us today!

JoLenaJohnson@absolutegood.com
Mission Possible Press is a Division of Absolute Good
PO Box 8039
St. Louis, MO 63156

The Aspiration Publishing Series will be successful and serve its purpose because you share your brilliance.

From my heart, mind and soul, thank you again!

Jo Lena Johnson, Be Inspired! Founder
Absolute Good Training & Life Skills Mgmt.,
Mission Possible Press
AbsoluteGoodBooks.com

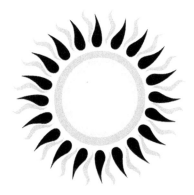

Even on Bad Hair Days, I am Brilliant!

I strive to do and be my best.
God handles the rest!

Yes, I am Brilliant!

Author Jo Lena Johnson Offers Inspiration and Solutions. She helps people learn how to communicate, lead, overcome conflict and build relationships through group & individual training sessions, seminars, coaching and workshops - personally and professionally. Communication is the Key!

Empowering individuals to be their best is what International Trainer & Speaker, Jo Lena Johnson specializes in through her consultancy, Absolute Good Training & Life Skills Management. *Offering Inspiration and Solutions* through her training, books and award-winning writing, she reveals tools and strategies for people to thrive and achieve in life, work, and relationships. Principle-focused, results-driven, and heart-centered, Jo Lena has taught over 85,000 people worldwide with her no-nonsense and dynamic approach.

Fast-paced and fun, her interactive self-discovery strategy sessions also help participants to develop skills in overcoming obstacles, build meaningful relationships and ultimately, achieve their goals.

In addition to hosting her Talk Show, *"It's Your Choice with Jo Lena Johnson,"* Jo Lena has been featured in The Voice, Urban Suburban, and Spirit Seeker Magazines; The St. Louis American Newspaper and on Good Day LA, Great Day St. Louis and various other television, radio and internet programs.

Get from where you are to where you want to be! Sometimes it's a matter of just knowing where to start, and of course, how to finish. Working with Jo Lena Johnson through classes, workshops, group and individual coaching sessions will give you the answers and solutions which are real and true for you. Publisher Jo Lena

Johnson also helps people tell their stories – by working with writers, turning them into published authors, with over 2 dozen books to date.

To schedule seminars, workshops, coaching, customized training or to bring Jo Lena to your organization, contact her at jolenajohnson@absolutegood.com or:

 JoLenaJohnson.com

 To follow her on LinkedIN
Jo Lena Johnson

 FACEBOOK
Jo Lena Johnson

 Twitter
@jolenajohnson

"Jo Lena Johnson is the voice of reason when you want to give up, the common sense in a world that sometimes does not make sense and the straight forwardness you need to have, when you are being coached for success!"

– N. Wallace

My Personal Notes

....

....

....

....

....

....

....

....

....

....

....

....

....

....

....

....

....

My Personal Notes

....
....
....
....
....
....
....
....
....
....
....
....
....
....
....
....
....

CPSIA information can be obtained
at www.ICGtesting.com
Printed in the USA
LVOW04s1229210316

480078LV00001B/40/P